MULTIPLICATION FUN PRACTICE BOOK

Multiplication Fun Practice Volume 1

Second edition, 2021.

Megageex.com

ISBN: 978- 965- 92743- 1- 4

TABLE OF CONTENTS

Marie Curie

Nikola Tesla

Charles Darwin

Isaac Newton

Jane Austen

Albert Einstein

FAIR USE OF THIS PRODUCT

At MegaGeex, we love making content designed to help build better learners. Our resources empower parents and educators alike to give kids hands-on inspiration to grow into the world-changing adults we want them to be. To be able to do that, we need your help to guarantee that we have the resources to continue to create great content.

If our resources are used beyond home and personal use, in a classroom, or other educational settings where you receive compensation, then a professional license is required.

Each professional license allows for a single teacher to use the resource for students in the teacher's class or block of classes. Price is determined by the number of students using the resource. If more than one teacher in your school wants access to the materials, then additional licenses are available for purchase.

Questions? Feel free to reach out to us at hello@megageex.com and we'll be happy to help. If someone you know would like to use one of our printable pages, have them check out www.megageex.com for our full catalog.

If we could look back over 600 years, most would be amazed at the developments, discoveries, and inventions that have changed the world. Human-kind, in this small space of time, has made advancements in every area of our lives. Communication is possible with people thousands of miles away- in real time! Circling the planet is accomplished in only days. Television, movies, computers, automobiles, only begin to tell the story of the mind-blowing improvements that benefit us all.

These awesome accomplishments were made possible by regular people who had extraordinary qualities. Men and women who shared two common traits: Passion and Grit. In the face of challenges and even failures, they never quit, and they succeeded in what many viewed as impossible.

With dedication and persistence, they overcame whatever hurdles given to them by society during their lives. Women such as Ada Lovelace, Marie Curie, and Jane Austen pursued their education despite laws and views that said they could not. George Washington Carver never gave up in the face of racial discrimination. And Albert Einstein could not find a job as a professor but he still continued work on his theories. These are just a few examples of the character of these remarkable individuals.

In 2018, Daniel Scalosub, embarked on a mission of his own. He wanted his twin daughters to know that they can do ANYTHING. And what better way to prove this to them than to share the incredible stories of these inventors, writers, scientists and artists, and entrepreneurs. Daniel founded Megageex to bring knowledge, and more importantly, inspiration and encouragement to kids everywhere.

Feel free to explore our unique products. Each one is designed with the sole purpose to inspire and teach through play and creativity.

Connect your kids with the world´s greatest minds and get ready for a learning journey like no other.

Welcome to Megageex!

MEET THE MEGAGEEX

NIKOLA TESLA

Serbian scientist, inventor, and futurist (1856 - 1942). Designed the alternating current (AC) model that provides electricity to homes. Pioneered radio transmissions and wireless technology.

ROSALIND FRANKLIN

English chemist (1920 - 1958). Proved the double-helix model of DNA, the building blocks of all life. Her work on the structure of viruses contributed to founding the field of structural virology.

THOMAS EDISON

American inventor and entrepreneur (1847 - 1931). Considered "America's greatest inventor". Invented the light bulb, the phonograph, the first motion picture camera, early electric power generators, and over a thousand other inventions.

GEORGE WASHINGTON CARVER

American agricultural chemist and agronomist (1860s - 1942). Developed methods for improving soil fertility, and crops versatility. Created products with peanuts, which gave him the nickname "the Peanut Man".

GALILEO GALILEI

Italian scientist (1564 - 1642). Considered the "father of modern physics". Pioneered the "scientific method" of learning through observation, asking questions and seeking answers by doing experiments.

THE WRIGHT BROTHERS

American aviation pioneers and inventors (Orville 1871 - 1948, Wilbur 1867 - 1912). They invented and built the first motorized airplane and were the first men to fly it in December 1903.

ISAAC NEWTON

English mathematician and scientist (1642 - 1727).
Formulated the laws of gravity, motion, and energy. Developed calculus, a new type of math for understanding and describing continuous change.

MADAM CJ WALKER

American businesswoman, entrepreneur, and social activist (1867 - 1919). Created the first cosmetics and hair care line of products for African-American women. First self-made American female millionaire.

WOLFGANG AMADEUS MOZART

Austrian composer and child prodigy (1756 - 1791).
Considered one of the most popular composers in western history, having composed more than 600 works. His music had a tremendous influence on subsequent western music.

ALEXANDER GRAHAM BELL

Scottish scientist, inventor, and teacher of the deaf (1847 - 1922). Invented the first practical telephone and founded AT&T, the world's first telephone company.

ADA LOVELACE

English mathematician and writer (1815 - 1852).
Regarded as the "world's first computer programmer". Wrote the first computer algorithm based on Charles Babbage's Analytical Machine.

CHARLES DARWIN

English naturalist and biologist (1809 - 1882). Pioneered the science of evolution. His work *On the Origin of Species* shows how beings evolve over time through natural selection.

HENRY FORD

American inventor and industrialist (1863 - 1947).
Started the Ford Motor Company and mass-produced the
Model T car. Developed the assembly line, which revolutionized
the factory production of goods in American industries. Influenced
the Labor Movement when he started the five-day/40-hour
workweek in his factories.

LUDWIG VAN BEETHOVEN

German composer (1770 - 1827). Began to lose his hearing at
age 28 and was deaf by age 45. It was during this time that he
created some of his greatest works. Considered to be one of the
greatest musical geniuses of all time and his most influential
works include the Eroica Symphony and Symphony No. 9.

ALAN TURING

English mathematician (1912 - 1954). Considered
the "father of computer science" and pioneered artificial
intelligence. Built early computers to break German codes
and help win World War II.

MARIE CURIE

Polish physicist and chemist (1867 - 1934). The
first woman to win the Nobel Prize for her discovery of
radioactivity, and the first person to win the Nobel twice.
Discovered the elements radium and polonium.

ALBERT EINSTEIN

German physicist (1879 - 1955). One of the world's
most influential scientists, whose work on light, gravity,
time and space changed the way we understand our
universe. Formulated the Theory of Relativity and Nobel
Prize winner in Physics.

Multiplication Table

Isaac Newton

Ada Lovelace

Alan Turing

X	1	2	3	4	5	6	7	8	9	10
1	1	2	3	4	5	6	7	8	9	10
2	2	4	6	8	10	12	14	16	18	20
3	3	6	9	12	15	18	21	24	27	30
4	4	8	12	16	20	24	28	32	36	40
5	5	10	15	20	25	30	35	40	45	50
6	6	12	18	24	30	36	42	48	54	60
7	7	14	21	28	35	42	49	56	63	70
8	8	16	24	32	40	48	56	64	72	80
9	9	18	27	36	45	54	63	72	81	90
10	10	20	30	40	50	60	70	80	90	100

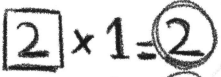

$2 \times 1 = 2$

$2 \times 2 = 4$

$2 \times 3 = 6$

$2 \times 4 = 8$

$2 \times 5 = 10$

$2 \times 6 = 12$

$2 \times 7 = 14$

$2 \times 8 = 16$

$2 \times 9 = 18$

$2 \times 10 = 20$

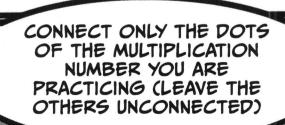

CONNECT ONLY THE DOTS OF THE MULTIPLICATION NUMBER YOU ARE PRACTICING (LEAVE THE OTHERS UNCONNECTED)

"A person who never made a **mistake** never tried anything new." ALBERT EINSTEIN "

Albert Einstein

Solution on page 64

Albert Einstein

15

"

Before you act, *listen*.
Before you react, *think*.
Before you spend, *earn*.
Before you criticize, *wait*.
Before you pray, *forgive*.
Before you quit, *try*.

ERNEST HEMINGWAY

"

The Wright Brothers

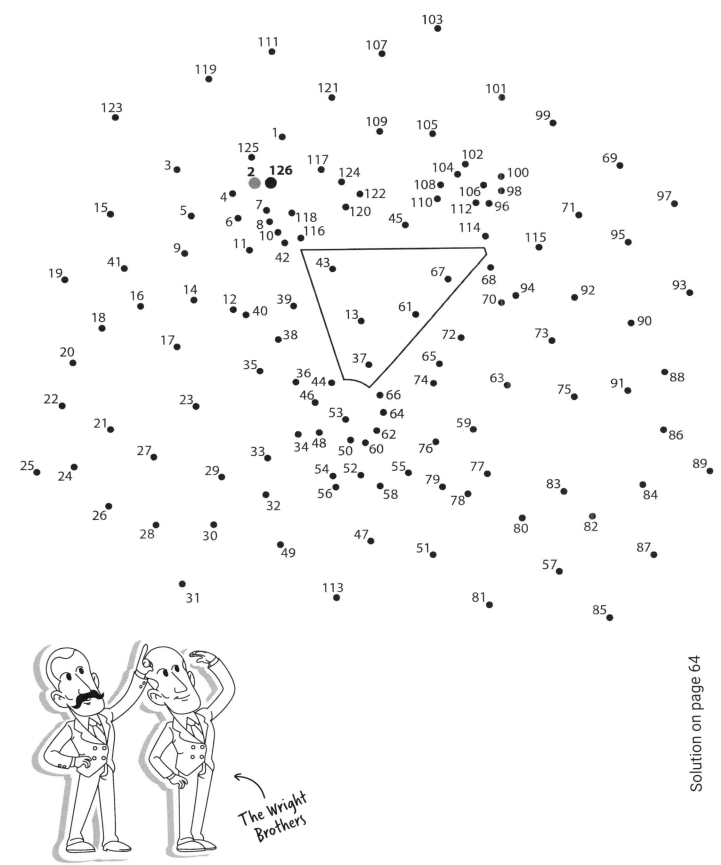

Solution on page 64

The Wright Brothers

"You miss 100% of the shots you

WAYNE GRETZKY "

Rosalind
Franklin

18

Rosalind
Franklin

Solution on page 64

"*Yesterday* is history. *Tomorrow* is a mystery. Today is a gift. That's why we call it **'The Present'**.

ELEANOR ROOSEVELT"

Wolfgang Amadeus Mozart

Wolfgang Amadeus Mozart

Solution on page 64

MegaGeex.com ©

"It always seems **IMPOSSIBLE** until it's done.

NELSON MANDELA "

Charles Darwin

22

Solution on page 64

Charles Darwin

"Believe you can and you're halfway there.

T. ROOSEVELT "

Alexander
Graham Bell

Alexander Graham Bell

Solution on page 65

"Determination is like a **muscle**. If you don't use it regularly, it **fades** *away*.

LYNN JENNINGS

Madam
C.J. Walker

Madam C.J. Walker

Solution on page 65

"A **_dream_** doesn't become reality through magic; it takes sweat, **determination** and hard work. "

COLIN POWERL

George Washington Carver

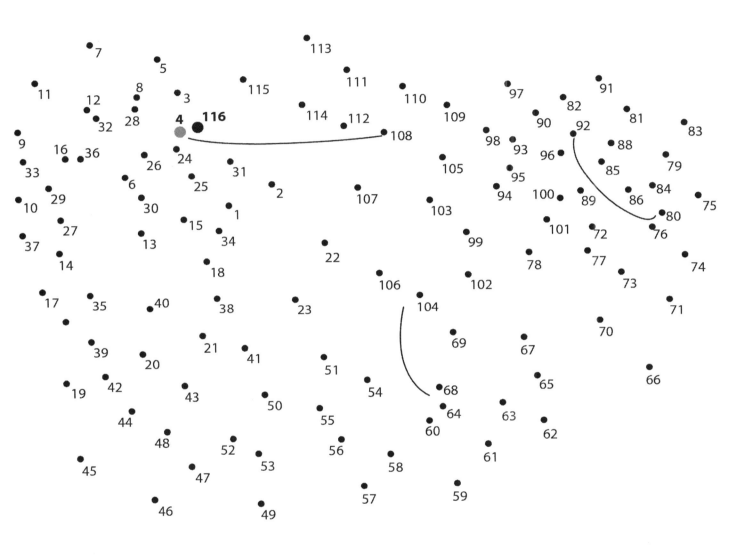

Solution on page 65

George Washington Carver

29

MegaGeex.com ©

"What we know is a dr💧p, what we don't know is an **OCEAN.**

ISAAC NEWTON 99

Isaac
Newton

Solution on page 65

Isaac Newton

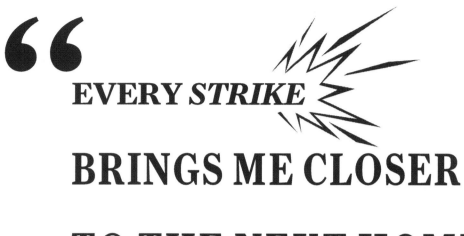

"**EVERY _STRIKE_ BRINGS ME CLOSER TO THE NEXT HOME RUN.**"

BABE RUTH

Galileo Galilei

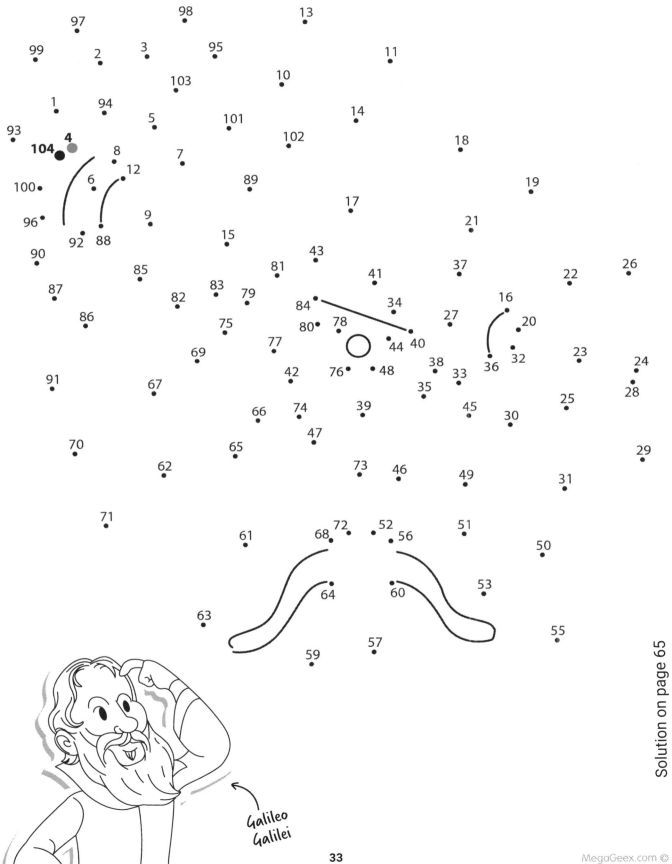

Solution on page 65

Galileo
Galilei

"You're braver than you believe, **STRONGER** than you seem, and *smarter* than you think."

A.A. MILNE/CHRISTOPHER ROBIN

Alan Turing

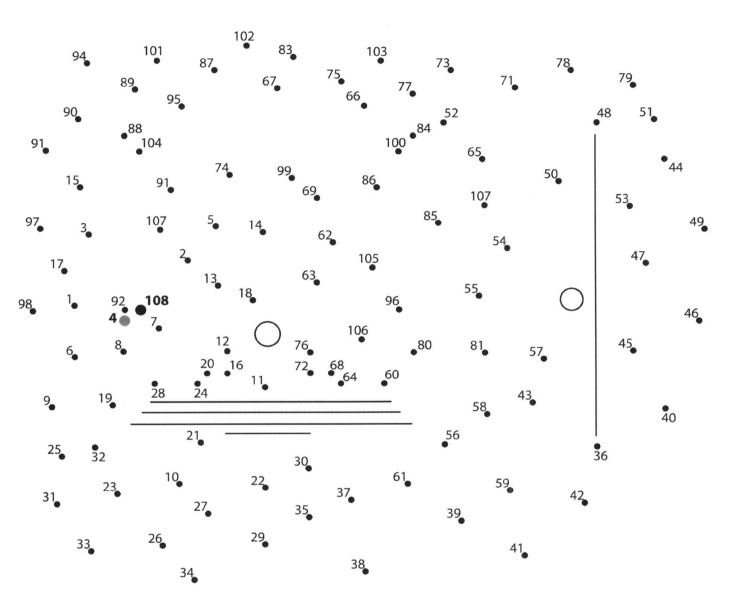

Alan Turing

Solution on page 66

MegaGeex.com ©

Genius is:

one percent inspiration and ninety-nine percent

PERSPIRATION.

THOMAS EDISON

Thomas Edison

36

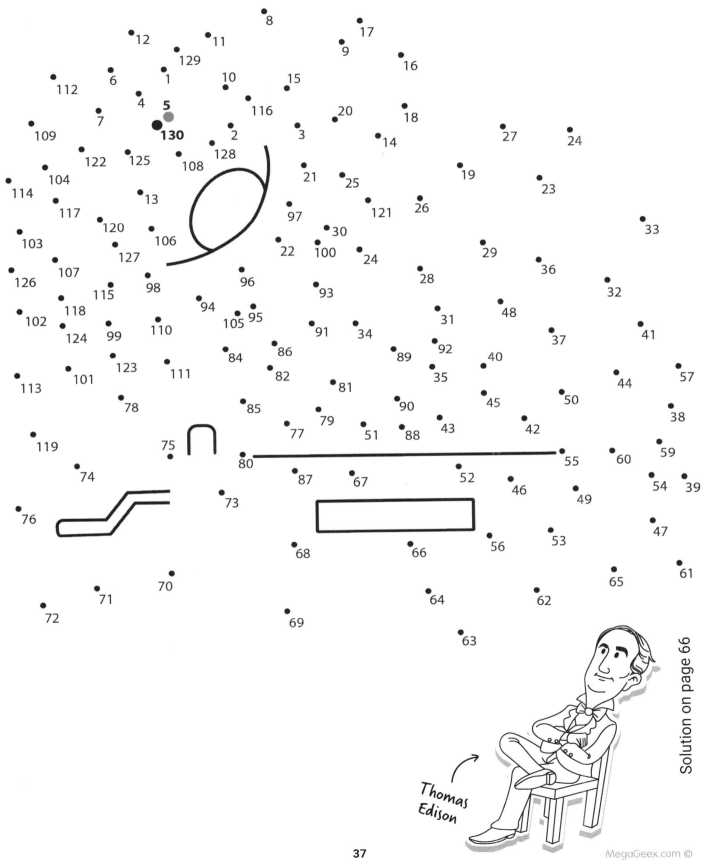

Thomas Edison

Solution on page 66

MegaGeex.com ©

"
All things are **difficult** before they are *EASY* "

THOMAS FULLER

Ada Lovelace

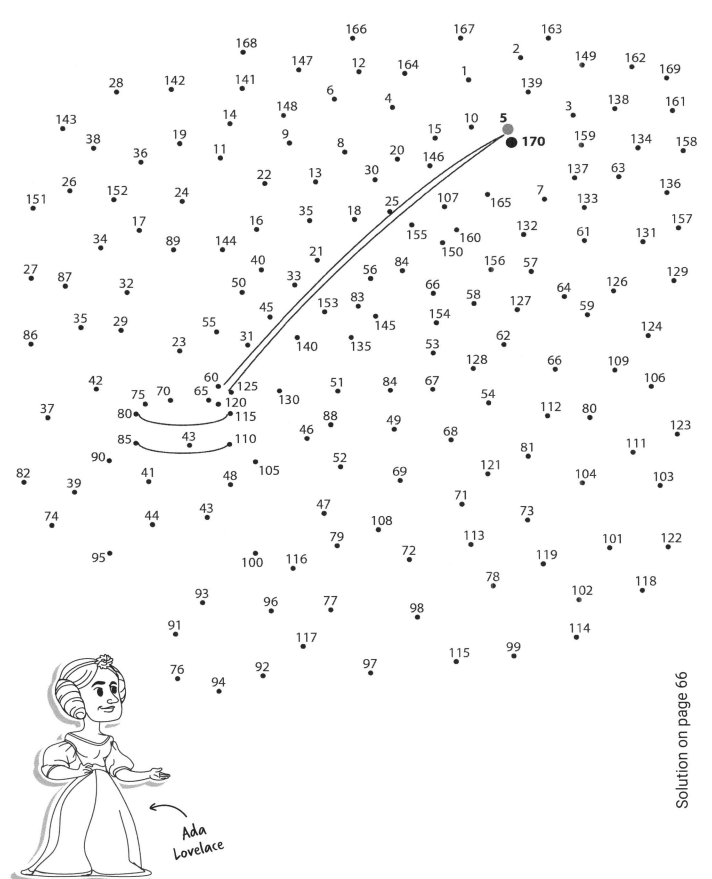

Solution on page 66

Ada Lovelace

"

Success is the ability to go from one failure to another with no loss of ENTHUSIASM.

WINSTON CHURCHIL

Marie Curie

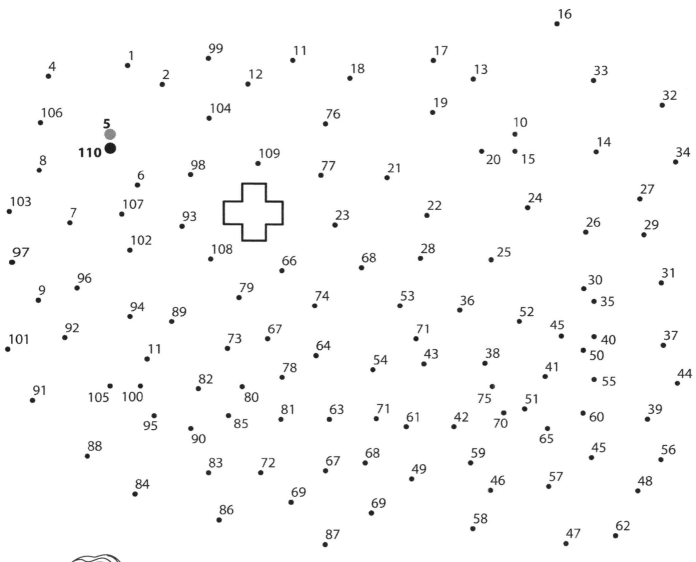

Marie Curie

Solution on page 66

MegaGeex.com ©

"The **more** that *you* read,
the **more** things *you* will know.
The **more** that *you* learn,
the **more** places *you*'ll go.

DR. SEUSS "

Nikola
Tesla

PRACTICE MULTIPLICATIONS OF 5

Nikola Tesla

43

Solution on page 66

MegaGeex.com ©

"It's not that I'm so **SMART**, it's just that I stay with problems **LONGER**.

ALBERT EINSTEIN "

Albert
Einstein

Solution on page 67

" I am 87 and I am still LEARNING. "

MICHELANGELO

Ludwig van Beethoven

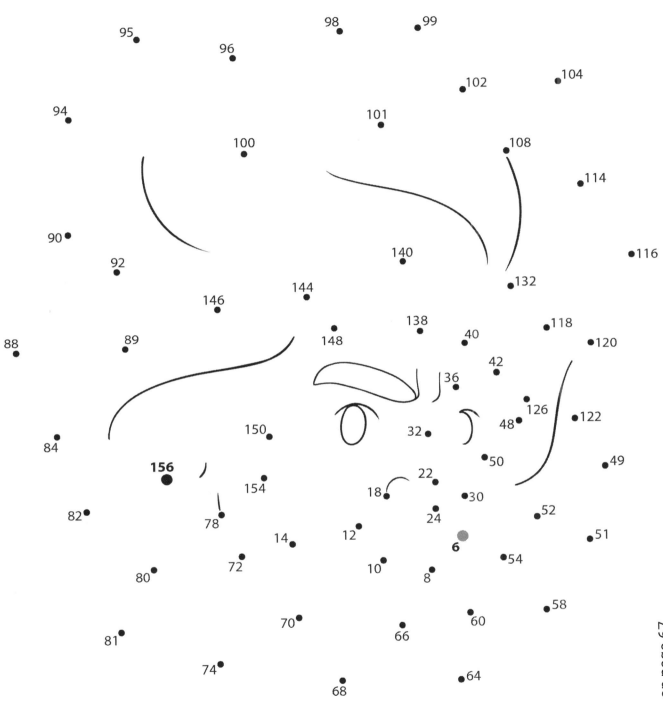

Solution on page 67

"The secret to getting *ahead* is getting *started*.

MARK TWAIN **"**

Rosalind Franklin

Solution on page 67

" Every problem is a gift. Without them we wouldn't GROW.

TONY ROBBINS "

Henry Ford

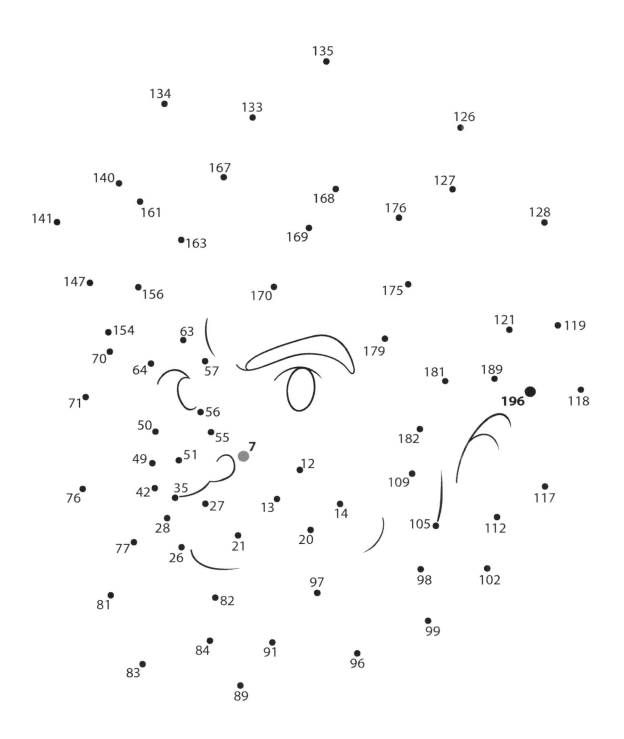

Solution on page 67

"Education is the key to unlocking the golden door to freedom.

GEORGE WASHINGTON CARVER "

George Washington Carver

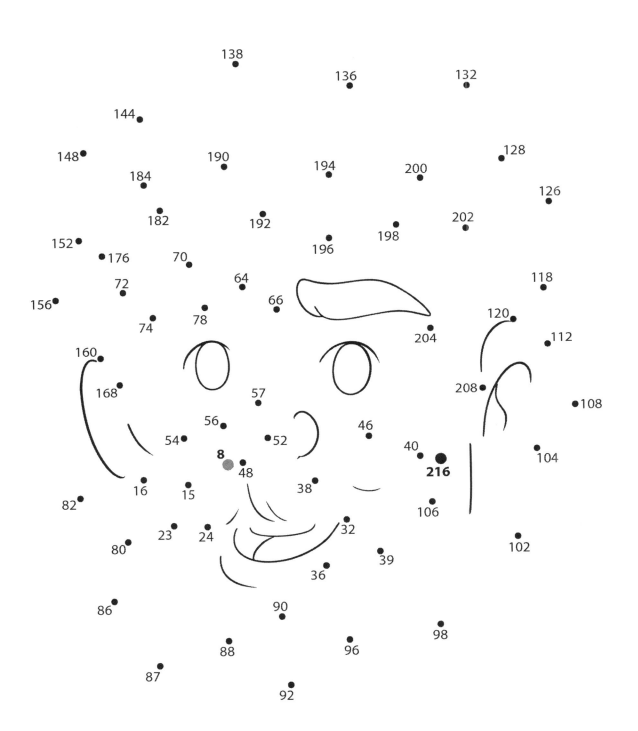

" It does not matter how slowly you go so long as you do NOT STOP. "

CONFUCIUS

orville Wright

Solution on page 68

"Always *DO* what you are *afraid* of doing.

RALPH WALDO EMERSON **"**

Wilbur Wright

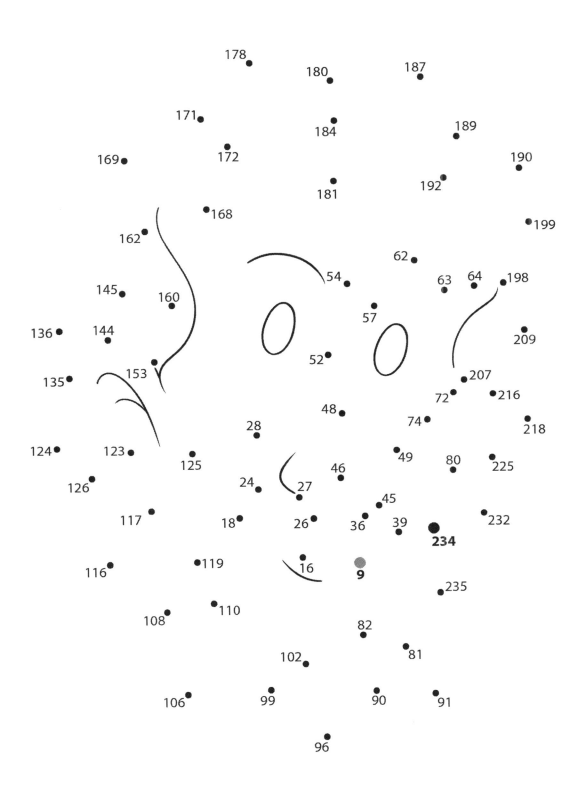

Solution on page 68

"

Take the first step in faith. You don't have to see the whole staircase, just take the first step.

MARTIN LUTHER KING

"

Isaac Newton

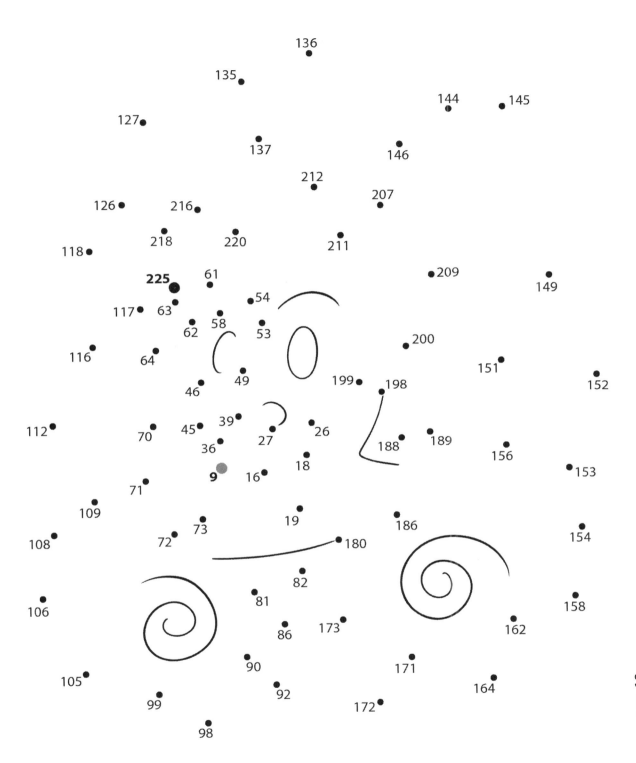

Solution on page 68

MegaGeex.com ©

" The best way to *predict* the future is to *create* it.

ABRAHAM LINCOLN "

Nikola Tesla

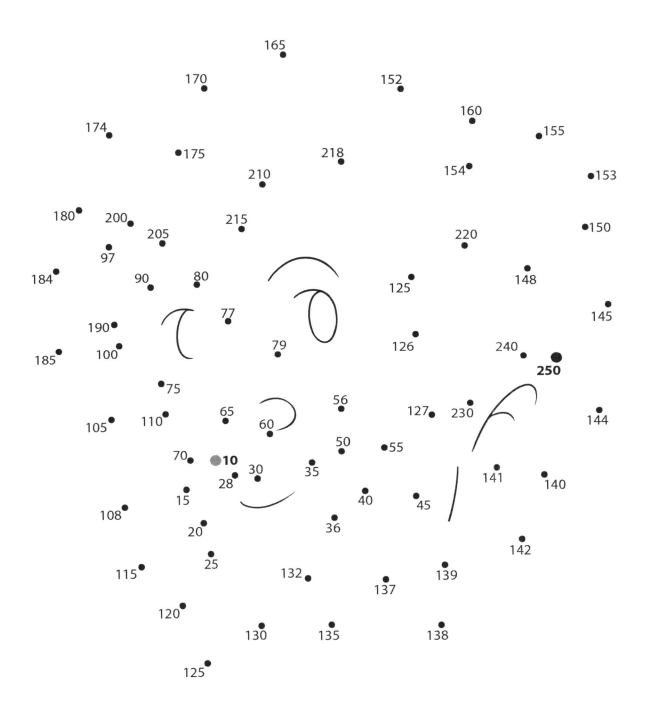

Solution on page 68

"Whatever you are, be a good one.

ABRAHAM LINCOLN "

Charles Darwin

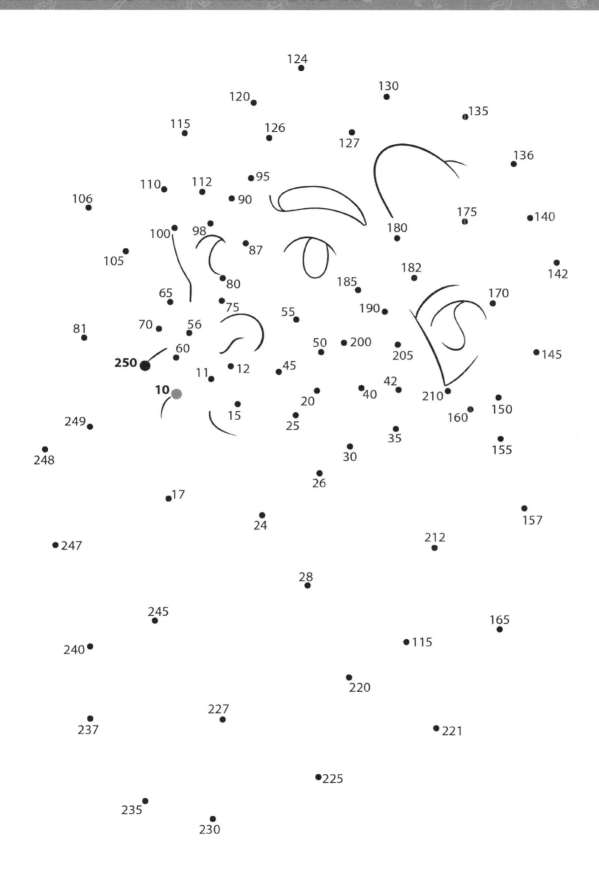

Solution on page 68

Page 15

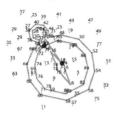

Einstein's Compass:

This object gave Albert Einstein's life direction, inspiring him as a boy to discover the natural forces which make up our universe.

Page 17

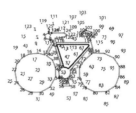

Bicycle

The Wright Brothers were avid mechanics and built bikes they designed themselves.

Page 19

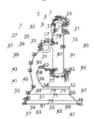

Microscope

Microscopes help us see very small things. They zoom in and let us see things like cells and viruses. Rosalind Franklin used microscopes to take pictures of DNA and polio viruses.

Page 21

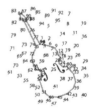

Violin:

A violin is an instrument with five strings. It is played with a bow, which also has strings. Mozart wrote many popular songs called concertos specifically for violin players. People like Albert Einstein loved to play Mozart's music even hundreds of years later!

Page 23

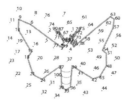

Butterfly

When Charles Darwin was a boy, collecting bugs was all the rage! He would collect butterflies and beetles and study them. Doing this helped him understand how they worked, and how they were similar and different from us.

Page 25

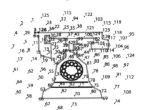

Original telephone

Many different inventors were working on ways to talk over long distances. Alexander Graham Bell invented and patented his first!

Page 27

Hot comb

A hot comb is used to straighten hair. Walker designed one that didn't do as much damage and cared for African-American women's hair.

Page 29

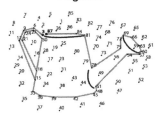

Watercan

Watering is very important for keeping plants alive. George Washington Carver worked very hard to teach everyone how to care for their plants, whether they had a small garden or a huge farm.

Page 31

Apple

One day when Isaac Newton was home from school, he saw an apple fall from a tree. Why did objects always fall to the ground? He had to know! Studying this helped him define the laws of gravity and motion, changing the world forever!

Page 33

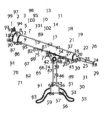

Telescope

Galileo used a telescope of his own design to see distant planets for the first time. He saw the moon, discovered that Jupiter had moons, and saw that Saturn had a ring!

Page 35

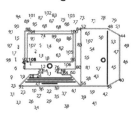

Computer

Computers make our lives easier by doing very advanced math. Some say they might be smarter than humans! Alan Turing developed a test to try out artificial intelligence. So far, no computer has passed the Turing Test!

Page 37

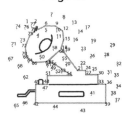

Phonograph

A phonograph records and plays sounds and was the first of its kind. Edison's creation of this made him famous, with people calling him "The Wizard of Menlo Park."

Page 39

Inkwell

Ink has been the main way people have written for hundreds of years. Before there were computers, Ada Lovelace wrote all of her works in ink, using only her mind, and wrote the world's first computer programs- in a book!

Page 41

Mobile radiography unit

Radiography units like x-rays allow doctors to see inside bodies. Marie Curie invented a mobile one during World War I, saving millions of lives!

Page 43

Electricity

Electricity powers our world, and Nikola Tesla helped make it so! He worked hard to make sure the world used alternating current to power homes, and said wireless electricity would be the future. Now we have wireless chargers for our computers and phones!

Page 45

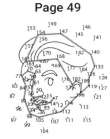

Albert Einstein

Einstein is considered one of the world's most outstanding scientists. However, he never learned to drive a car. Also, he loved to sail, but he never learned to swim.

Page 47

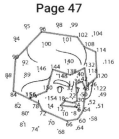

Ludwig van Beethoven

When Beethoven's hearing began to worsen, he would place a reed between his teeth and touch the keyboard with the reed. He could feel the vibrations of each note.

Page 49

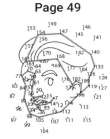

Rosalind Franklin

Famous for her discovery of the structure of DNA, many don't know that her previous work studying coal led to the development of safer gas masks for soldiers.

Page 51

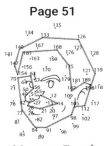

Henry Ford

As a child, Ford's father gave him a broken watch. He fixed it. He then began fixing watches for friends and neighbors. If he didn't have the correct tool for a repair, he would make the tool himself.

Page 53

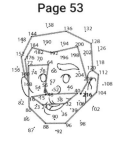

George Washington Carver

George is best known for his work as an agricultural scientist and inventor. But, he could also play the piano, accordion, and mouth harp. Further, he was a talented painter.

Page 55

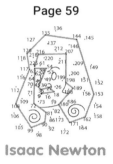

Orville Wright

For the first flight, the brothers flipped a coin to decide who flew first. Wilbur won the coin toss but his attempt at flying failed. Orville went next and flew the plane for 12 seconds.

Page 57

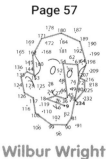

Wilbur Wright

A toy helicopter ignited a passion in the Wright Brothers for things that fly. Wilbur and Orville even built a life-size version of the toy.

Page 59

Isaac Newton

Albert Einstein once said that Isaac Newton was the smartest person who ever lived.

Page 61

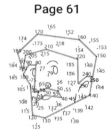

Nikola Tesla

Nikola Tesla had an incredible memory. He memorized books, diagrams, plans for inventions, and he spoke seven languages.

Page 63

Charles Darwin

Charles Darwin attended university to become a doctor. However, he thought watching surgeries was gross. So he left medical school.

Puzzle Instructions

1. Cut the puzzle pieces

24   15   56

2. Solve the multiplication quiz questions

3. Glue the pieces in the quiz page according to your solutions

8x7   6x4   3x5

PRACTICE, PRACTICE, PRACTICE... MAKES EVERYTHING LOOK EASY :)

"

All your *dreams* can come true if **YOU** have the *courage* to pursue them.

WALT DISNEY "

Nikola
Tesla

$1 \times 6 = \underline{\quad}$

$2 \times 6 = \underline{\quad}$

$3 \times 6 = \underline{\quad}$

$4 \times 6 = \underline{\quad}$

$5 \times 6 = \underline{\quad}$

$6 \times 6 = \underline{\quad}$

$7 \times 6 = \underline{\quad}$

$8 \times 6 = \underline{\quad}$

$9 \times 6 = \underline{\quad}$

$10 \times 6 = \underline{\quad}$

Solution on page 131

Follow your heart and ignore the noise.

No matter what Tesla did, people were always talking about him—sometimes good, sometimes bad. Just like Tesla, you decide how you act, no matter what other people say.

> "Whether you think *you* can or you think *you* can't, **you're right**.
>
> HENRY FORD "

Rosalind
Franklin

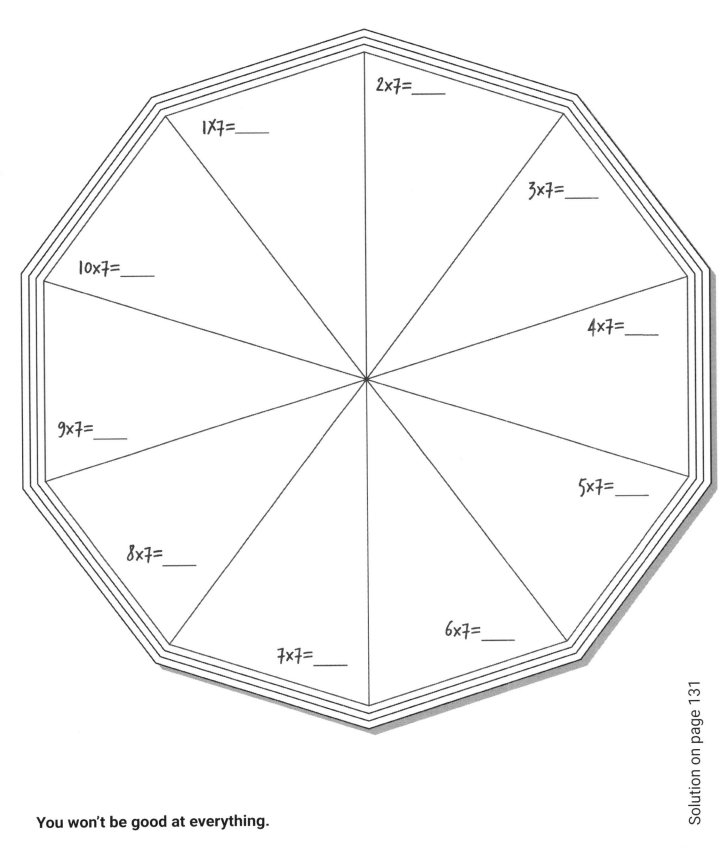

2x7=___

1x7=___

3x7=___

10x7=___

4x7=___

9x7=___

5x7=___

8x7=___

6x7=___

7x7=___

Solution on page 131

You won't be good at everything.

Rosalind Franklin's music teacher thought she must have a hearing problem she was so bad! Focus on what skills you do have, and how you can improve them.

"The most certain way to succeed is **always** to try just *one more time...*

THOMAS EDISON

Thomas Edison

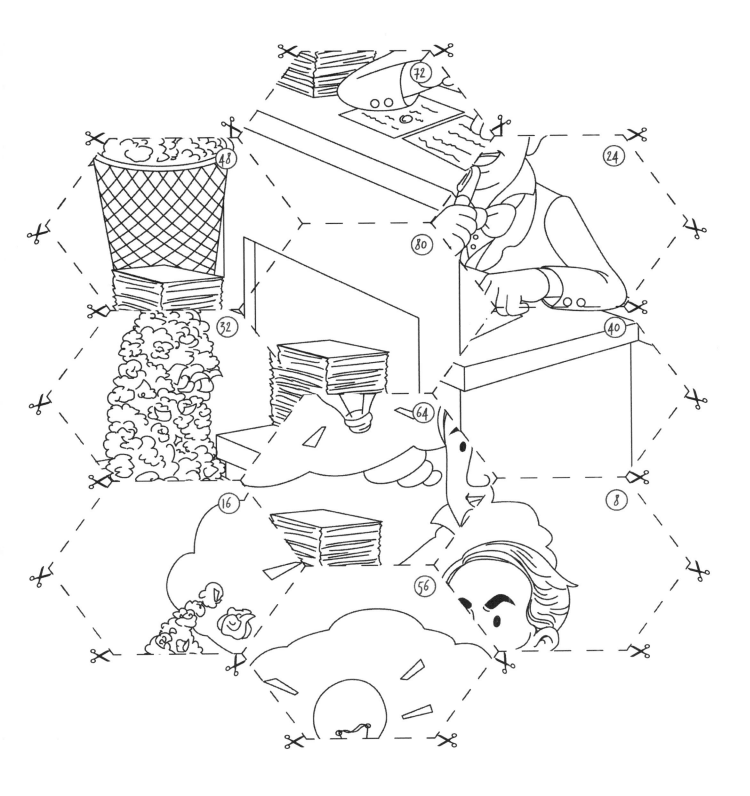

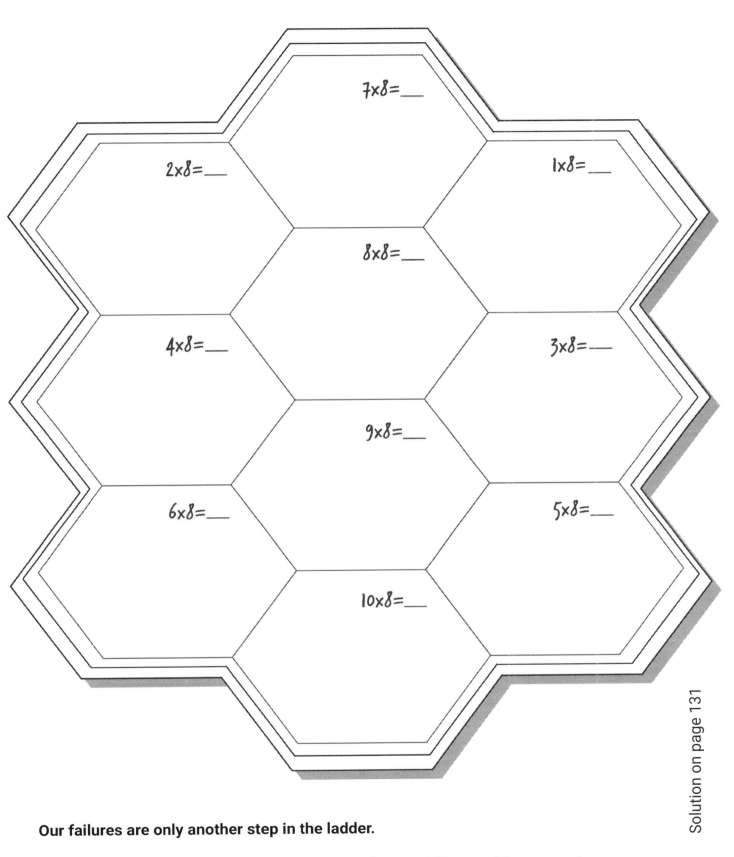

7x8=___

2x8=___

1x8=___

8x8=___

4x8=___

3x8=___

9x8=___

6x8=___

5x8=___

10x8=___

Solution on page 131

Our failures are only another step in the ladder.

After his first invention failed to sell, Thomas Edison said he would never make something that couldn't be sold. Learn from your failures and plan for the future!

MegaGeex.com ©

Obstacles don't have to stop you.
If you run into a wall, don't turn
around and give up.
Figure out how to *climb it,*
go through it, or work around it.

MICHAEL JORDAN

George
Washington
Carver

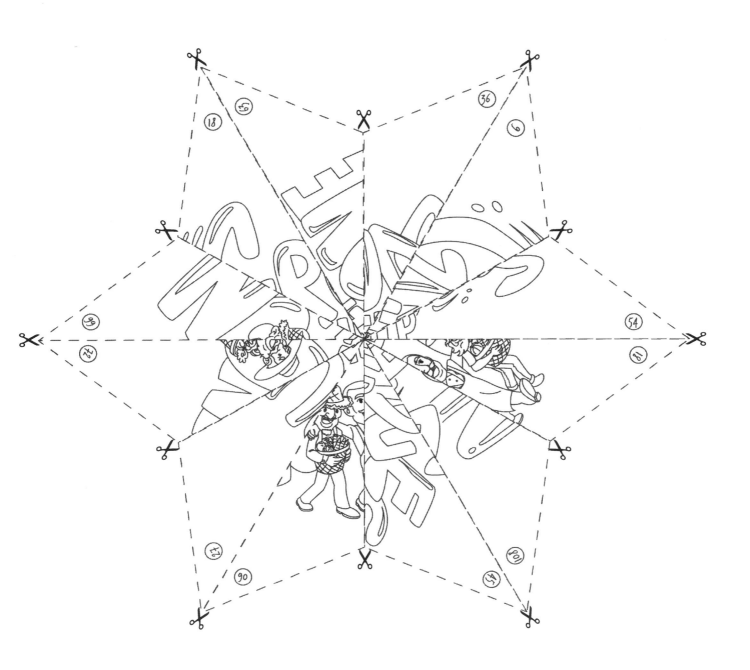

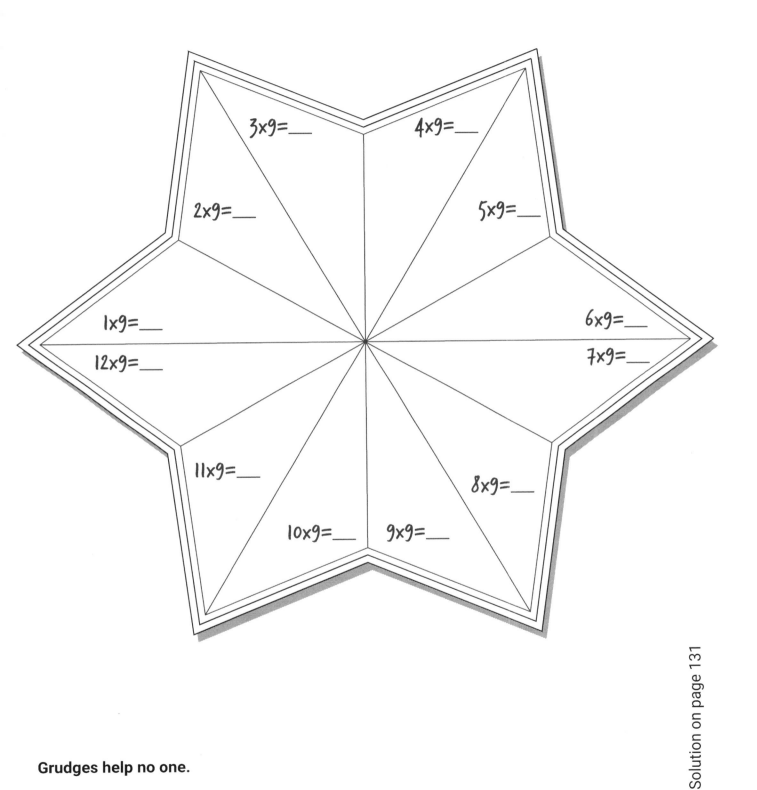

Solution on page 131

Grudges help no one.

No matter how mean people were to him, George Washington Carver never held a grudge. Many people tried to stop him from learning because he was black, but after he was an expert, he traveled the country helping everyone, black or white.

MegaGeex.com ©

"

Courage is not the absence of *fear*,

but the TRIUMPH over it.

NELSON MANDELA "

Galileo
Galilei

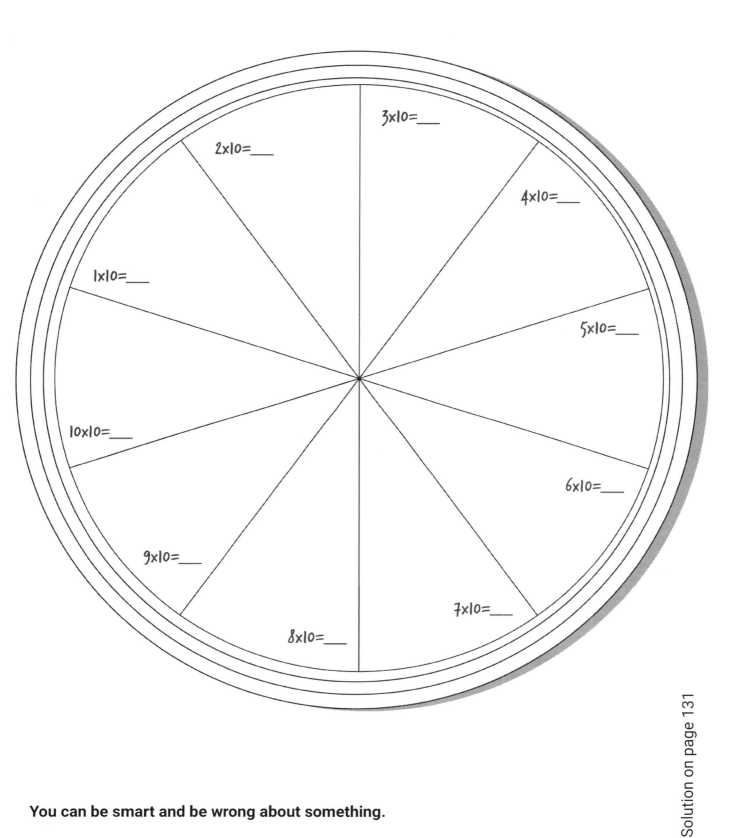

3x10=___

2x10=___

4x10=___

1x10=___

5x10=___

10x10=___

6x10=___

9x10=___

7x10=___

8x10=___

Solution on page 131

You can be smart and be wrong about something.

Though he was brilliant, Galileo Galilei was not right about everything: he did not think the Moon caused the high and low tides of the water on Earth! You can be brilliant and wrong at the same time.

"Nothing is particularly hard if you **break it down** into small jobs.

HENRY FORD "

The Wright Brothers

4x2=___   5x3=___   8x5=___   8x7=___   1x9=___

2x3=___   6x4=___   7x3=___   9x6=___   10x7=___

Solution on page 131

Learn from your elders.

Learn from your parents and guardians! Though they got their curiosity from their father, the Wright Brothers learned to repair and build things from their mother.

"If I have seen further than others, it is by standing upon the *shoulders of* GIANTS. "

ISAAC NEWTON

Isaac Newton

1x8=	2x7=	3x6=	4x5=	5x6=	6x9=	7x5=	8x4=	9x3=	10x10=
___	___	___	___	___	___	___	___	___	___

Solution on page 131

Your skills may surprise even you.

A well-known scientist, Isaac Newton was also rather sneaky: he discovered a secret group of counterfeiters making fake coins and spent years tracking them, before having them arrested in the name of the King.

"Why fit in when you were born to STAND OUT?"

DR. SEUSS

Wolfgang Amadeus Mozart

$7 \times 9 =$ ___	$8 \times 7 =$ ___	$7 \times 1 =$ ___	$10 \times 10 =$ ___
$2 \times 12 =$ ___	$5 \times 14 =$ ___	$1 \times 1 =$ ___	$1 \times 11 =$ ___
$5 \times 9 =$ ___	$3 \times 5 =$ ___	$8 \times 8 =$ ___	$3 \times 4 =$ ___
$9 \times 9 =$ ___	$9 \times 10 =$ ___	$7 \times 6 =$ ___	$6 \times 9 =$ ___

Solution on page 131

Find your comfort zone.

When Mozart was 22, he was sent by his father to become famous in Paris, but he was out of his comfort zone and didn't know French. Though he was technically gifted, Mozart couldn't pull off his fame, yet. It's ok to have setbacks, you'll get there in the end.

"Perseverance is **failing** 19 times and succeeding the 20th.

Madam C.J. Walker

$6\times7=$ ___	$7\times7=$ ___	$8\times5=$ ___	$5\times9=$ ___
$10\times5=$ ___	$2\times5=$ ___	$9\times9=$ ___	$9\times8=$ ___
$5\times4=$ ___	$5\times5=$ ___	$10\times9=$ ___	$4\times7=$ ___
$2\times9=$ ___	$3\times3=$ ___	$4\times8=$ ___	$1\times8=$ ___

Solution on page 131

You have to chase success.

Madam C.J. Walker believed that success was something everyone could do, but that you had to get out there and chase success! Success is not something that happens to you, it's something you achieve by doing!

MegaGeex.com ©

"If you get *tired*, learn to *rest* not to quit."

BANKSY

Alexander Graham Bell

1x1=___	7x14=___	10x10=___	6X6=___
5X5=___	1x20=___	5x16=___	6X15=___
4X4=___	2x19=___	8x13=___	9X9=___
3X3=___	3x18=___	9x12=___	8X8=___
2X2=___	4x17=___	10x11=___	7X7=___

Solution on page 132

Fun drives our passion.

Alexander Graham Bell set a world record with a speed boat he created for fun.
Sometimes fun is the first step to our passions!

"**Success** is not final,
FAILURE is not fatal.
It is the courage
to continue that counts."
WINSTON CHURCHILL

Charles
Darwin

11X2=___	7X2=___	8X4=___	5X5=___
17X4=___	11X9=___	12X8=___	9X5=___
14X5=___	15X8=___	16X9=___	13X4=___
6X3=___	19X3=___	20X10=___	17X2=___
2X8=___	3X7=___	4X6=___	1X9=___

Solution on page 132

Keep your mind sharp.

Throughout his life, Charles Darwin suffered from a mysterious illness that kept him sick most days, but he didn't let that stop him! He had a strict regimen to keep his mind sharp and his body working.

113

If you can't make a mistake, you can't make ANYTHING.

Ada Lovelace

11x6=___

2x4=___

3x8=___

1x1=___

5x10=___

6x8=___

7x3=___

5x14=___

9x6=___

10x8=___

11x5=___

8x7=___

15x6=___

16x9=___

19x2=___

12x8=___

Solution on page 132

Don't let others limit your vision.

Many people thought computers were only for crunching numbers, but not **Ada Lovelace!** She thought they could create music, write poetry, and connect people. Your vision can make all the difference.

"Everything you can imagine is real.

PABLO PICASSO **"**

Alan Turing

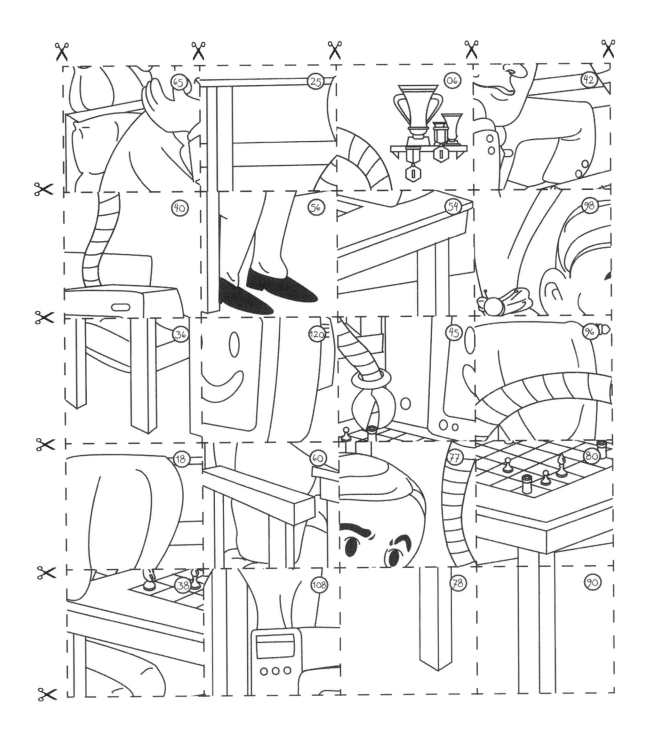

3x6=___	5x5=___	8x12=___	2x3=___
7x14=___	7x11=___	9x12=___	4x10=___
5x13=___	6x7=___	3x15=___	10x12=___
4x15=___	2x19=___	2x40=___	3x18=___
6x6=___	8x7=___	9x10=___	6x13=___

Solution on page 132

Invent for fun.

In his spare time, Alan Turing looked for fun ways to use computers. He invented the first chess program, which is one 1of the first video games!

"Everything is within your *POWER*, and your *POWER* is within you.

JANICE TRACHTMAN "

Marie
Curie

MegaGeex.com ©

5x16=____

4x17=____

2x19=____

3x18=____

1X20=____

11x2=____

12x3=____

10X11=____

7x14=____

8x13=____

9x12=____

6X15=____

17x8=____

18x9=____

19x10=____

16X6=____

14x5=____

15x7=____

13X4=____

5x8=____

16x2=____

13X7=____

15x4=____

7X4=____

The letter S in Success stands for Struggles.

While Marie Curie studied in Paris, she would collapse in the cold winter streets because she was too poor to buy food. On cold days, she used to wear ALL her clothes at night so she wouldn't freeze. Brrrr....

Solution on page 132

MegaGeex.com ©

"The important thing is to not stop questioning. **CURIOSITY** has its own reason for existing.

ALBERT EINSTEIN

Albert
Einstein

126

2x2=___	3x8=___	4x10=___	9x13=___
8x7=___	3x17=___	5x19=___	4x8=___
7x11=___	6x12=___	5x5=___	10x10=___
3x18=___	8x14=___	15x3=___	20x4=___
20x9=___	15x8=___	12x7=___	12x4=___
14x2=___	14x7=___	14x3=___	11x6=___

Solution on page 132

Serendipity will change your life.

When Einstein was five, he was given a compass by his father, and later said this gift inspired him to study physics. Inspiration can come from the smallest things - always be open to inspiration!

Page 71

Page 75

Page 79

Page 83

Page 87

Page 91

Page 95

Page 99

Page 103

Page 107

Page 111

Page 115

Page 119

Page 123

Page 127

Finished the book?
Well done!

Send us a video and receive a
certificate diploma from Megageex!
support@megageex.com

How can you get more
out of MegaGeex?

Subscribe to our newsletter at
www.MegaGeex.com and follow us on
Instagram and Facebook
to receive free activity pages to inspire
your kids.

🌐 www.MegaGeex.com

📷 MegaGeex

f MegaGeexCom